INSTANT
GOALS

Instant Goals

The INSTANT-Series *Presents*

INSTANT

GOALS

How to Set Goals and Achieve Them
Instantly!

Instant Series Publication

ISBN 978-1-508-88236-7

Printed in the United States of America

First Edition

FIRST STEP:

Before proceeding, visit http://www.instantseries.com, and join the **INSTANT Newsletter** now.

You will want to! :)

Instant Goals

CONTENTS

Chapter 8 - Start Your Goals Now

<u>Chapter 1</u>

Importance of Goal Setting

You Must Set Goals

To achieve anything worthwhile in this world, you need to **set goals.**

You're probably sick of hearing this piece of advice from your parents and grandparents, who've said it to you a thousand times. And you're probably frustrated that no one ever tells you *how* to set goals, just that you need to.

They always end up telling you a story about some guy who worked hard to make it big. How does it help you to know that the Mexican billionaire Carlos Slim struggled through his life and become the business magnate he is today through perseverance and determination? Can't they come up with something more practical instead of this overly talked about success story?

Wouldn't it be more helpful to have a personalized guide to goal achievement rather than hear about other people's success stories?

Success Vs. Goal

Everyone, *more or less,* wants the same thing in life: To be successful in whatever you do.

There's no time for inspirational cookie-cutter success stories. Instead, you want what works for you and is effective with **immediate results.**

And we can all agree that if you don't express your wants and desires through objectives or goals, you'll just end up going through the motions of life, and in 10 years from now, when you look back at what you've done, you'll wish it had been more fulfilling.

Let's face it. In our society, you cannot be **successful** without doing some kind of leg work; there are often many obstacles to tackle before you can achieve greatness. The key to overcoming these obstacles is to turn them into **goals**. Anybody can do this and achieve greatness.

This is not about trying to change your nature. It's about using practical principles to identify your needs. It might seem a bit simplistic at first, but you'll see that it's worth your time.

What Does Success Mean To You?

The goal here is not to bombard you with useless common sense, which you probably already know anyway, but, rather, it's to direct your attention to what others don't do.

Now let's elaborate on this. **Goal setting** is very personal because it concerns making important life decisions that apply specifically to you and your objectives.

Everyone is different and some people will achieve success faster than others. The added pressure that comes with seeing others *"get there"* before you do, and wishing that you had more time, or that you had more passion so you can be successful like *"them,"* can affect you negatively. And while you do need **passion** to succeed, remember that it's all about you. So try to focus on you and don't compare yourself to others during this process.

To start, think about what you want to leave behind as your legacy.

Now, let's dig deeper into setting your goals and implementing them.

Chapter 2

How to Set Goals the Right Way to Easily Achieve Them

Be Realistic

Let's start with pointing out the core of the **problem** here.

The biggest mistake people make when setting goals is **setting unrealistic ones.** Stop reaching for the stars, and star with changing little things in your life.

In other words, the reason why people have difficulty achieving their goals is because the goals they've set for themselves are beyond their **personal realities.**

The Wrong Way To Set Goals

Imagine, if you will, a thirty-something woman who has decided, for the first time in her life, to purchase a new car. Aside from it being her primary mode of transportation, the car will also make her feel more independent. She really wants an expensive car with prestige, like a BMW M5 convertible, which costs over a hundred thousand dollars to purchase, and will probably run her over $1,500 dollars per month.

The problem is this woman lives in New York City, rents an apartment with two friends, and works as a waitress in a restaurant for $10 an hour.

Now, one might think *"She can get financing for the car from a bank,"* and, yes, she can get financing. And there's nothing wrong with wanting to buy a car or loving luxurious things.

But, here's the problem...

Not only should she have picked a cheaper car, but she apparently doesn't understand that the choice she has made will put her under so much **stress**—much more stress than catching the train every morning for a single job paying $10 an hour.

Now, here's the **cautionary tale**: this woman will most likely be in debt for a very long time, and because she's of an age in which certain things are expected of her, she may think that she has to prove herself to the world. She'll purchase the car in spite of her current financial situation then do something crazy, like try to get another job to pay for it.

Inevitably, all of this will lead to her going to work late because she had a late-night shift at her second job, or not being able to pay her bills. Neither situation turns out good for her because either her car will be repossessed because she can't afford it, or she will lose her waitressing job...*you know*, the one where she was earning $10 per hour!

So as you can see, she's back to square one: No car and, to make it worse, no job.

That is the unfortunate result of not knowing **how to set up your goals**.

Goals go hand-in-hand with **priorities**. It is important that you ask yourself what your priorities are and what you really need.

Also, you must set up priorities that help you **move forward**. The intention here is to always move forward, and to never find yourself back at square one, like our woman with the too expensive car.

<u>Exercise</u>: Prioritize Yourself

Your first assignment is to keep a notebook of all your priorities. As you think of new ones every day, write them down in the notebook.

Here are some <u>guidelines</u>:

1. Write down everything you need to do in the next 6 months.

2. Then, make a list of everything you want or desire to have by the end of the year.

3. Now, organize the two lists under different headings; for example, *"wish list," "projects," "investments,"* etc.

4. After you've organized the lists, evaluate the cost of each item, in terms of money and time.

5. Then, think about what you earn and compare it to what you spend or may spend each month. Weigh all the items against your monthly budget and eliminate

the ones that go beyond what you can afford, either in terms of money or time.

6. Now, keep the ones that fit within your budget—items that, once you pay all your bills and necessities, won't leave you scrambling before your next payday.

Set In Motion

Now what do you have left?

You have left a list of things that you want and can achieve during the next 6 months. The good news is you can extend your time span up to a year, which is perfect because it's **realistic** and **clear**.

By following these guidelines, you have eliminated any financial constraints and given yourself the necessary time (from tomorrow *till* 6 months later, or a year).

With that done, let's move on to the next step.

Chapter 3

Immediately Achieve Your Short-Term Goals Now

The Instant Gratifications

Short-term goals are typically goals you want to achieve within the next day or couple of months, so they should be easy to reach, *right?*

The answer is *not necessarily*, and anyone who has failed to accomplish short-term goals knows the reality behind it.

Short-term goals should be taken seriously. Not only because it might concern something crucial, like continuing your education, or losing weight for health reasons, but also because you want to eliminate them from your list effectively, *right?*

It is also important that you take enough time to really make the distinction between what needs to be done immediately and what can be done later.

<u>Task</u>: Set Your Short-Term Goals

Here's what you should do first:

1. Define your short-term goals. From your **previous exercise**, you should know by now that goals need to be quantified and completed within a specific time frame.

2. Keep the ones that you can afford, time-wise and financially. Regroup the goals into specific time frames: what you can achieve within the *next few days*, weeks, and 6 months.

After you've defined your short-term goals, now comes the time to set them. Set them effectively by following these <u>guidelines</u>:

1. *As discussed earlier,* you must be concise and clear. Group your goals into different categories. For instance, financial goals would be grouped under the heading *"Savings,"* goals pertaining to wants or needs would be grouped under *"Wish List,"* and goals that don't require a financial commitment would be grouped under *"To Do List."*

2. Now give each goal a value. It has to be measurable so that it is palpable, and adds more gravitas to what you want to achieve. Consider, for instance, someone who wants to lose weight. This person's New Year's resolution was to lose enough weight so that she could look like Halle Berry. *How is she going to do it? Does she have to know Halle's eating habits?* No, it wouldn't be fair to try to eat like a Hollywood star, so she should forget about that part. Instead, she should set a weight loss goal for a month, by stating that she will lose 20 pounds over the next few weeks. Here we have a value for the goal and the time needed to accomplish it. So remember, always quantify your goal. It makes it **more concrete**, in other words, more real.

3. Don't flood yourself with too much to do all at once. Meaning that you shouldn't set more than **5 goals** at once during the same day or week. Instead, try to spread them out over the entire month. This will maximize your chances of working on them effectively.

4. Give yourself enough time to complete your goals. This point is very crucial in achieving your short-term goals. If you don't give yourself enough time to complete them, you'll never get anywhere. This is why it is crucial to span your short-term goals from a day *to up to* 6 months.

5. Give yourself enough resources to accomplish your goals. It is important that you be specific when you evaluate the amount of effort and resources you will need to reach your goals, because you must prioritize these resources in order to accomplish anything. Your main resources are **time** and **money**.

6. Rank your goals from *least complex* to the *most complex*. Considering that the most complex of them are either time consuming or demand a lot of financial sacrifice *(i.e. saving)*, start with the least complex ones, so that it will allow you to devote more time and resources to the others.

Staying Motivated

Another aspect of short-term goal setting is **motivation**.

How do you stay motivated through this whole process?

It is quite simple.

First of all, don't talk about your plans, or what you are currently trying to accomplish to anyone. Keep it to yourself until you actually reach that goal.

The reason for this **discretion** has to do with other people's insecurities and tendency to criticize what they don't know or understand.

Keeping Track

The second tip to staying motivated is to <u>keep a journal</u>.

In that journal, write down a checklist and check off all the goals that you are achieving progressively.

Write down all your challenges and comments about what you've learned in the process.

This will motivate you and even help you discover new aspects of your personality that will help you do better, work faster, and move forward.

Chapter 4

Set Bigger Long-Term Goals to Achieve

The Big Fishes

You should know first-hand that **long-term goals** take more time and need more preparation and sacrifice than your short-term goals.

Now because long-term goals are more *time consuming* and, consequently, have more *complex objectives*, you should consider giving them a time frame of <u>at least a year</u>.

If you want to effectively achieve your long-term goals, you have to be more methodical in the process of labeling and grouping them. It's more involved than what you have already done with your short-term goals, but you can do it if you proceed in the following manner.

Task: Set Your Long-Term Goals

Group your long-term goals into different categories, *in addition* to labeling them and allocating a value to each one of them.

The categories should be directly linked to the number of years needed for realization.

For instance, let's say you want to achieve the following long-term goals:

- Buy a house
- Send your 5-year-old child to a private school
- Save money for retirement

- Save money for your next vacation
- Save money for a luxury bag
- Save money for your wedding

Now what should you do?

You should ask yourself which **one** of the 6 goals has the most urgency?

You can see clearly that your child's education should be the most important on the list because she's of an age when she should be entering Kindergarten soon.

Hence, this goal should be in the <u>1 year category</u>.

Next, you should ask yourself which ones are the most costly and, in turn, need more time to save up?

Saving for **retirement** and **buying a house** should fall under this category, and should be put in the <u>10 or more years category</u>.

Saving for your **wedding** is just as costly, but you don't want to wait 5 years before you get married, so it should fall under the <u>2 years category</u>.

Lastly, saving for an **expensive luxury bag** and your **vacation** should fall in the <u>1 year or a year-and-a-half category</u>.

With this plan, you are putting aside a set amount of money each month for the house that you plan on buying in the next 15 years as well as for your retirement, and you'll also have money for your child, your bag, and your vacation.

Once you've achieved these last 3, you'll even have more money for your wedding, and so on.

Don't Overload On Long-Term Goals

Do you see how a **methodical categorization** makes things easier and more precise?

Now, for your plan to be effective you have to remember not to add new priorities to the ones that will take <u>1 to 2 years</u> on your list.

People who do that end up doing nothing because they lose focus and become overwhelmed about which goal to work on first.

Striving to fulfill a need that takes a very long time takes a lot of courage and, most of all, faith.

These two characteristics are necessary in order to remain motivated to complete the tasks at hand.

Work In Progress

Don't be afraid to **document** yourself when pursuing long-term goals that will take you 10 or more years to achieve.

Seek out professionals and ask them questions. For instance, when saving to buy a house, be informed about the latest regulations and laws. By doing this, you'll feel closer to your end goal.

Also, keep a **journal** of your long-term goals, and keep notes about how things are progressing.

And most of all, always **visualize** the gratifications that will come with accomplishing these crucial goals, such as a well-educated and successful child, a beautiful and inviting home, and a stress-free and relaxing retirement.

At the end of the road, there will definitely be a sense of **self-accomplishment**. Always keep in mind that the choice you've made to set responsible goals separates you from those who have no goals.

Chapter 5

Goal-Setting Activities

Implementation Time

Now that you have learned how to set your goals, try to implement what you've learned.

Exercise 1: Your Top 15

1. Write down your top **15 priorities**.

2. Organize your priorities from the *least costly* to the *most costly*.

3. Then, group your priorities into two categories: *less time consuming* and *more time consuming*.

Exercise 2: Turn Your List Into Goals

Take the lists you've created and turn them into goals.

- For your less time consuming or short-term goals, divide the list into specific categories and label them. (for example, Wish List, Finances, etc.)

- For your more time consuming or long-term goals, do the same thing, but also rank them according to how long it might take you to reach them.

Exercise 3: Test Your Understanding

Answer the following questions:

1. How long should it take you to achieve a long-term goal?

A.) 1 year

B.) 3 months

C.) 2 weeks

D.) All of the above

2. Buying a $1000 jacket should be:

A.) A long-term goal

B.) A priority

C.) A fantasy

D.) None of the above

3. My motivation for moving forward should be found in:

A.) Friends and family

B.) My researches and investigations

C.) At church

D.) All of the above

4. Long-term goals should be treated like short-term goals as long as they're easy to attain.

A.) True

B.) False

5. As long as you're motivated, you should add more resolutions to your list. Motivation alone should push you forward.
A.) True
B.) False

Exercise 4: Plan Your Days

You will need a journal or notebook for this exercise.

Assess yourself after one week of working on your goals:

- What went well?
- What went wrong?
- How would you rate yourself?
- What can you do in order to improve yourself?

How do you effectively work on your short-term goals on a daily, weekly, or monthly basis?

From now on, plan your days the nights before by prioritizing the shortest goal(s) in terms of time *(or money)*. Make sure that in your plan you have given the goal the appropriate time span.

Differentiate this goal(s) from the rest of the things that you do daily by writing it in a different color, like red ink.

Remember to write down the exact steps that you will take. In other words, write down how you are going to proceed. *For example*, if you plan on enrolling at a university, write down the time that you wish to get there and the department you want to go to.

Next, pin that list on a bulletin board in your room, on your fridge, and in your organizer *(whether it's electronic or in paper form)*. There will never be an excuse for you not to remember what you **"have"** to do when you step out of your house.

After the first week of working on a goal, assess your efforts—*make notes about what happened while you were trying to attain that goal.*

Now in addition to the guidelines you already have, do the exact same thing for every short-term goal that you have in mind.

Remember, setting these goals on paper is 50% of the job, so don't freak out. Because if you can materialize them on paper, you can excel at them in practice.

Chapter 6

Putting It All Together

Short-Term Goals In Action

Here's a clearer step-by-step explanation of how you should proceed:

Imagine you are planning to learn a new language online, let's say French.

After you decide which online learning option best fits you, plan out your days as follows:

Week 1

- <u>Day 1</u> - Pay the fees and familiarize yourself with the different learning options offered *(beginner, intermediate, advanced, etc.)*.

- <u>Day 2</u> - Get to know the learning site and begin your first online class. Don't forget to have a notebook so you can take notes.

- <u>Day 3</u> - Take 20 minutes to practice before you log on to the learning site, then log on and proceed with your class.

- <u>Days 4 & 5</u> - Do the same thing *(because this is your first week of learning)*. You'll get to know the language better by applying the same routine.

- <u>Day 6</u> - Take your first language quiz for beginners and test your knowledge. Assess yourself and note your weak points.

- <u>Day 7</u> - Take a break!

Week 2

- <u>Day 1</u> - Practice and focus on your weak points for **30** minutes before class.

- <u>Day 2</u> - Practice and focus on your weak points for **20** minutes before class

Do the exact same thing for <u>Days 3, 4 & 5</u>.

- <u>Day 6</u> - Take another quiz to test your knowledge. Assess yourself and note your weak points like you did in the first week.

- <u>Day 7</u> - Rest.

Now, observe the same routine for **weeks 3 and 4.** Remember, you can learn a new language in 2, 3, or 6 months depending on your learning abilities. Just make sure you follow these steps.

By the end of the **first month**, assess yourself with another online test covering what you've learned throughout the month.

If you fail the test, give yourself 3 days, and devote 3 hours a day to practicing *(take a 20 minute break every hour)*.

Retake the test after 3 days. When you pass *(and you will)* apply the same routine to the next learning level, which, in this case, would be intermediate, and then advanced.

Don't forget to complement you learning sessions with additional research as you progress, like renting a French film *(for word recognition)*, ordering an easy-to-read French book, or reading a French article online from time to time.

Do you see how strategic and simple it is to work on short-term goals?

Long-Term Goals In Action

Using an **organizer,** plan all of your long-term goals together. But this time, spread them out to 1 year, 2 years, 5 years, and so on. Then, plan them over a *weekly, monthly, or yearly* basis.

Here again, write down how you are going to proceed.

For instance, if you are setting a **financial goal,** plan it on a monthly basis. Decide the amount you want to deposit every month, and on what date you will make that deposit every month.

If you're planning a **wedding,** determine the steps you need to follow so that everything turns out the way you want it to—write down the costs, schedule your appointments, etc., all in your organizer.

If you're planning to **buy a house,** locate the type of house you want, visualize the neighborhood, and decide on a price range.

Always have a calendar and determine which goal should be reached by the end of the first year. Mark it in a bright color, like red.

Dedicate enough time to all of your long-term goals. Since you can't start working on them all at once, start with the ones that take shorter than 5 years to accomplish and plan your activities around them on a weekly basis.

Every time you're done with your weekly activities, check them off and start with the next ones. And don't forget, these activities directly relate back to the progress you're making on your long-term goal.

Long-Term Goal Extended Example

Pay attention to the following example of a typical long-term goal: **a wedding**.

Imagine you are getting married in one year. Opt for a weekly to a monthly plan of preparation.

Week 1

- <u>Day 1</u> - Start making calls and inquiries about costs, decorations, and other items that you might need for a wedding.

- <u>Day 2</u> - Arrange your costs into categories (wedding dress $1500, venue for celebration $5000, administrative costs $1000, the number of people to be invited, cost of food, etc.).

- <u>Day 3</u> - Get out and visit your chosen locations, such as wedding venues, bridal shops, etc.

- <u>Day 4</u> - Check off all the things you've done so far on your list and rest for the day.

- <u>Days 6 & 7</u> - Rest.

Week 2

- <u>Day 1</u> - Make some more calls and inquiries.

- <u>Day 2</u> - Compare your new costs to the old ones. Arrange them into categories.

- <u>Day 3</u> - Visit your chosen locations, including more wedding venues and shops.

- <u>Days 4, 5, 6 & 7</u> - Follow the same steps you had for **week 1**.

Weeks 3 and 4 should be filled with the same activities.

By the end of the first month, you should have a better idea of your total budget, the type of wedding dress you want, your venue, and the number of people you are inviting.

With that in mind, your plan will continue to take shape in **month 2,** as decisions begin to get made and financial obligations sorted out.

Week 1

- <u>Day 1</u> - Inquire about venue booking and payment plan for the wedding dress.

- <u>Day 2</u> - Go ring shopping with wife or husband to be.

- <u>Day 3</u> - It's time to choose the cake. Try as many wedding cakes as possible, and bring your mom or sister to have a third party's opinion.

- <u>Day 4</u> -Discuss your accomplishments with your partner.

- <u>Day 5</u> - Decision day, where you will discuss and decide how much you want to spend, and each other's participation in terms of finance, wedding ring costs, etc.

- <u>Days 6 & 7</u> - Rest.

Week 2

- <u>Day 1</u> - Start working on your finances (you should have an estimate of the total budget by now). If you want to get financing for some of the expenses, start calling banks.

- <u>Day 2</u> - Decide with your significant other how much each one of you should put aside every 2 weeks to pay the wedding costs.

- <u>Days 3 & 4</u> - Make calls to more banks.

- <u>Day 5</u> - Compare the rates offered by financial institutions and decide which one is the most appropriate for you and your partner.

- <u>Days 6 & 7</u> - Rest.

Week 3

- <u>Day 1</u> - Start saving and transfer your contributing percentage to a shared account.

- <u>Days 2, 3 & 4</u> - Discuss the layout, decoration, organization, and possible vendors.

- <u>Days 5, 6 & 7</u> - Rest.

Week 4

- <u>Day 1</u> - With members of your family, brainstorm more about the ceremony and reception.

- <u>Day 2</u> - Visit the venue where you want your wedding to take place, and start thinking about how best to setup the layout *(chair, tables, stage, etc.)*.

- <u>Day 3</u> - Make a wish list of decorations, flowers, colors, etc., to submit to your wedding coordinator.

- <u>Day 4</u> - Share your wishes with family members and gather information that could help you.

- <u>Days 5, 6 & 7</u> - Rest.

By the end of **month 2**, check off everything on your list that you have accomplished. Also, calculate the money that you have collected and compare it to your total budget, so that you know how much you still have to save.

Month 3 *all the way to* **month 6** should focus on the <u>financial part</u>:

<u>Days 1 & 5</u> *(Mondays and Fridays)* of months **3, 4, 5, and 6** should be focused on financial deadlines *(in terms of contributions)* and keeping up with any changes, like regulations *(vendors, venue, etc.)*.

By **month 6,** you should evaluate all that you've accomplished, including vendor contracts and financial obligations, so that you know what's left to be done.

Months 7 and **8** should be about putting everything together.

Month 7, Week 1

- <u>Day 1</u> - Start rehearsing with the officiant.

- <u>Day 2</u> - Try on your dress and make any adjustments, if necessary. Also, make initial payment.

- <u>Days 3 & 4</u> - Rest.

- <u>Day 5</u> - Send invitations to all your guests, and suggest an RSVP.

- <u>Day 6</u> - Start choosing the menu, linens, decorations, etc.

- <u>Day 7</u> - Rest.

Continue checking that everything is going along smoothly, at least during **week 2** and **week 4** of **month 7**.

Month 8, Week 1

- <u>Day 1</u> - Start making payments for the venue and other vendors (caterer, DJ, photographer, etc.).

- <u>Day 2</u> - Finalize payments on your dress.

- <u>Days 3, 4, 5, 6 & 7</u> - Rest.

For the remainder of **weeks 2, 3,** and **4,** rest.

There shouldn't be much to do during **month 9**.

Month 10 should be about yourself:

Week 1

- <u>Day 1</u> - Get a gym membership, so that you can look flawless in your dress.

- <u>Day 2</u> - Attend a 1-hour workout.

- <u>Day 3</u> - Visit a spa for a foot or body massage.

- <u>Day 4</u> - Shop for your honeymoon.

- <u>Day 5</u> - Book your honeymoon.

- <u>Days 6 & 7</u> - Rest.

Continue, *more or less*, with the following schedule for the remaining weeks:

- <u>Day 1</u> - Work out at the gym.

- <u>Day 2</u> - Work out again.

- <u>Day 3</u> - Visit a spa for a foot massage or body massage.

- <u>Days 4, 5, 6 & 7</u> - Rest.

In **month 11,** we are approaching the big day:

Week 1

- <u>Day 1</u> - Finalize all remaining payments (venue, food, photographer, etc.).

- <u>Day 2</u> - Finalize the layout of the venue and acknowledge the final setting.

- <u>Day 3</u> - Last rehearsal with the officiant.

- <u>Day 4</u> - Try your dress on one last time to see if

everything is still okay and make adjustments if
necessary.

- <u>Day 5</u> - Rest.

- <u>Day 6</u> - Get your dress, bring it home with you.

- <u>Day 7</u> - Rest.

Week 2

- <u>Day 1</u> - Take a final look at the guest list, and make
sure everyone who replied yes has a seat at your
reception.

- <u>Day 2</u> - Make an appointment with a hairstylist and
make-up artist.

- <u>Day 3</u> - Have your rings delivered to the best man.

- <u>Day 4</u> - Have the bridesmaids and groomsmen

outfits delivered.

- <u>Day 5</u> - Late bills and last minutes adjustments of the week.

- <u>Days 6 & 7</u> - Rest.

Week 3

- <u>Day 1</u> - Call the wedding coordinator to check if there's anything missing. If yes, fix it.

- <u>Day 2</u> - Check with the bridesmaids and groomsmen to see if they need accommodations near the venue.

- <u>Day 3</u> - Make sure you and your partner's dress and suit are ready and stored.

- <u>Day 4</u> - Rest.

- <u>Day 5</u> - Plan your bachelor/bachelorette parties.

- <u>Day 6</u> - Have your bachelor/bachelorette parties.

- <u>Day 7</u> - Rest.

Week 4

- <u>Day 1</u> - Finalize how the venue will be setup and decorated.

- <u>Day 2</u> - Check if the hairstylist and make-up artists are still available.

- <u>Day 3</u> - Go to the venue and check that everything is there and ready for the big day *(freezers, tables, chairs, etc.)*.

- <u>Day 4</u> - Invite the wedding party to come to your house for one last meeting before the big day.

- <u>Day 5</u> - Pay the make-up artists and hairstylist.

- <u>Day 6</u> - Have decorative items and beverages delivered and stored at the venue.

- <u>Day 7</u> - Rest and prepare for the big day because you've covered everything!

Chapter 7

When You Lose Your Way: How to Stay Motivated to Continue the Fight

Utilize Your Setbacks

This is the part that everybody hates. Ninety percent of the time when you are trying to accomplish an objective, something **distracts** you and leads you away from your goals.

Do you remember that girl or guy in high school that everybody used to like *(especially you)*?

You couldn't help but think about him or her all the time, and you watched their every move. But they never even knew you existed. The two of you, obviously, never became a couple (certainly not from a lack of trying, though) and, at the time, you were devastated and felt like a failure. But now when you look back, you realize that this rejection was the springboard that helped you blossom into the person you are today. In fact, it may have even helped you find better partners throughout your life.

The point is, even though this person wasn't your partner, you learned from the experience, and through time, you were able to apply what you learned and have better, more meaningful relationships.

The difficulties you encountered in high school inspired you to work harder the rest of your life.

So when you become distracted and start to lose motivation, keep the following in mind:

- You are moving forward from now on.

- Goal setting will help you upgrade your way of life.

- Setting your goals means that you know what you want in life, and achieving them makes you a grown *man/woman*.

- And lastly, challenges make life more exciting. Wouldn't it be boring if everything was easy? *How would you learn?*

Just Keep Moving

Most of the time rock stars' performances are out of this world, but sometimes things go a little wonky, like a wardrobe malfunctions or someone's singing goes off-key. But these rock stars don't give up when bad things happen. Not only do they have a reputation to maintain, but also they know that at the end of the day they'll receive an enormous payout, both financially and in the positive feedback they'll receive from the media for handling their failures like pros.

You should think of yourself like that rock star and handle your *"failures"* like a pro: Don't give up, and look for **feedback**.

Now what kind of feedback are you looking for?

Well, feedback, *in your case*, will surface when you go through all the steps and note what you haven't done or could do better.

Always consult yourself first before asking for other people's advice.

Assess Yourself In Between

Read through your notes; check that you haven't ignored a step, or forgotten something. And don't forget to constantly **assess** yourself. **Constant assessment** keeps your undertaking alive and, above all, motivates you.

Let's say you are raising funds for a charitable event. Here's an example of an assessment after a week's worth of work:

- <u>Day 1</u> - Distribute pamphlets in schools, factories, and corporations.

- <u>Day 2</u> - Distribute pamphlets in train stations and malls.

- <u>Day 3</u> - Set up appointments with local radio stations to announce your event and ask for donations.

- <u>Day 4</u> - Advertise your event online through social media.

- <u>Day 5</u> - Make calls to the schools, factories, and corporations to ask if they are willing to donate to your event.

- <u>Day 6</u> - Assessment day: How much did you raise in the first week? What went wrong? How well did you do? What could you do better the next time?

- <u>Day 7</u> - Rest.

<u>Exercise</u>: **Start On Your First Goal Now**

1. Grade yourself on your **first task:** How much progress have you made toward accomplishing your first goal (*long-term* or *short-term*)?

2. Rate the rest of your goals according to complexity (*for example, saving for a house has a rating of 80% difficulty*).

3. Visualize how you will approach or counteract these complexities.

Now, how do you feel after the visualization process?
Doesn't it feel like you've already done half the work
toward achieving your goals?

Chapter 8

Start Your Goals Now

Don't Get Discouraged

Setting goals and achieving them can be very tricky, and it's easy for someone to get discouraged throughout the process.

When you see your friends and family improving their lives while you struggle to achieve even the smallest goal, it makes you feel left out, like everyone is part of this elite club that you'll never get an invitation to. The **pressure** of *"keeping up with the Jones's"* can get to you and make you not want to see your goals through to the end.

But, *hopefully by now*, you'll realize that you don't need to be a genius or follow an intense spiritual cleansing in a remote area to renew your sense of purpose.

All you need to do is something you already know how to do, which is *"handle your own business."* Always look to your own faculties and capabilities first before you start seeking help from others, because *you* have the ability to self-motivate and commit to your own engagements. Don't compare yourself to others and don't rely on others to achieve your goals for you.

Setting goals and implementing a plan to achieve these goals are crucial aspects of *"handling your own business."*

What are You Waiting For?

Everyone wants a nice life filled with cars, houses, and an education that leads to better opportunities, but these nice things don't just happen, and you don't get anything *extra*ordinary without putting in the *extra* work!

Thankfully, goal setting doesn't impede on your everyday life. All it takes is a little bit of **time** and **focus**.

So what are you waiting for?

Grab a pen and put yourself to work. Start making changes in your life and be **proactive** in creating the future that you want, and deserve. Achieve your goals today for a better tomorrow!

Good luck!

An INSTANT Thank You!

Thank you for entrusting in the <u>INSTANT Series</u> to help you improve your life.

Our goal is simple, help you achieve instant results as fast as possible in the quickest amount of time. We hope we have done our job, and you have gotten a ton of value.

If you are in any way, shape, or form, dissatisfied, then please we encourage you to get refunded for your purchase because we only want our readers to be happy.

If, *on the other hand*, you've enjoyed it, if you can kindly leave us a review on where you have purchased this book, that would mean a lot.

What is there to do now?

Simple! Head over to http://www.instantseries.com, and sign up for our **newsletter** to stay up-to-date with the latest instant developments *(if you haven't done so already)*.

Be sure to check other books in the INSTANT Series. If there is something you like to be added, be sure to let us know for as always we love your feedback.

Yes, we're on **social medias.** *Don't forget to follow us!*

https://www.facebook.com/InstantSeries

https://twitter.com/InstantSeries

https://plus.google.com/+Instantseries

Thank you, and wish you all the best!
- *The INSTANT Series Team*

Manufactured by Amazon.ca
Acheson, AB

12897983R00042